Why do snakes slither?

Miles Kelly

First published as Why Why Why in 2007 by
Miles Kelly Publishing Ltd, Harding's Barn,
Bardfield End Green, Thaxted, Essex, CM6 3PX, UK

Copyright © Miles Kelly Publishing Ltd 2007

This edition published 2010

2 4 6 8 10 9 7 5 3 1

Editorial Director **Belinda Gallagher**
Art Director **Jo Brewer**
Assistant Editor **Lucy Dowling**
Volume Designer **Sally Lace**
Cover Designer **Jo Brewer**
Indexer **Hilary Bird**
Production Manager **Elizabeth Collins**
Reprographics **Anthony Cambray,
Liberty Newton, Ian Paulyn**
Editions Manager **Bethan Ellish**
Character Cartoonist **Mike Foster**

All artwork from the Miles Kelly Archives

ISBN 978-1-84810-168-5

Printed in China

British Library Cataloging-in-Publication Data
A catalog record for this book is available
from the British Library

Made with paper from a sustainable forest

www.mileskelly.net
info@mileskelly.net

www.factsforprojects.com

Contents

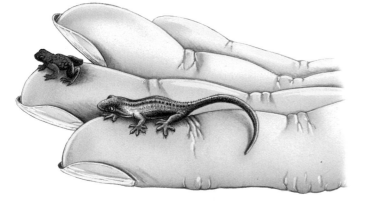

What is a reptile?

Python

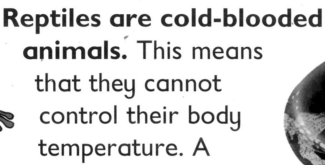

Reptiles are cold-blooded animals. This means that they cannot control their body temperature. A reptile's skin is dry and scaly. There are four kinds of reptile—snakes and lizards, crocodiles and alligators, tortoises and turtles, and the tuatara, a kind of lizard.

Why do reptiles sunbathe?

Reptiles do a lot of sunbathing! This is called basking, and they do this to get warm so that they can move about. When reptiles are cold they find it difficult to move quickly.

Discover

Next time you are on the beach, bury your legs in the sand to feel how cool it is.

What is an amphibian?

Amphibians are cold-blooded animals. Most amphibians live in or around water. The skin of an amphibian is smooth and wet. The main groups of amphibians are frogs and toads, newts and salamanders, and caecilians.

Eastern newt

Head in the sand!

Some amphibians, such as the spadefoot toad, live in very hot places. If it gets too hot, the spadefoot toad buries itself in the sand to cool down!

Cane toad

Why do frogs cross the road?

When spring arrives, amphibians come out of hiding. It is time for them to have their babies. Many amphibians return to the pond or stream where they were born. This may mean a very long journey through towns or over busy roads to breeding grounds.

Frogs

6

When do amphibians sleep?

When the weather turns cold, amphibians often hide away. They hibernate (go into a deep sleep) under stones and logs. This means that they go to sleep in the fall, and don't wake up until the next spring!

Mind the frog!

In some places road signs warn drivers that frogs and toads are traveling along the roads to return to their breeding grounds.

Hibernating toad

Can lizards dance?

When the sand gets too hot, the sand lizard of the African Namib Desert performs a strange dance. It lifts its legs up and down off the burning sand or lies on its stomach and raises all its legs at once!

Explore

In the fall, have a look under some stones and logs for sleeping frogs—try not to wake them!

Why do amphibians lay eggs?

So that their babies can hatch. Amphibians lay eggs in water. Frogs and toads lay a jellylike string or clump of tiny eggs called spawn. Newts lay one egg at a time. Some amphibians give birth to live young that are born looking like tiny adults.

1. Frog spawn

2. Tadpoles hatch

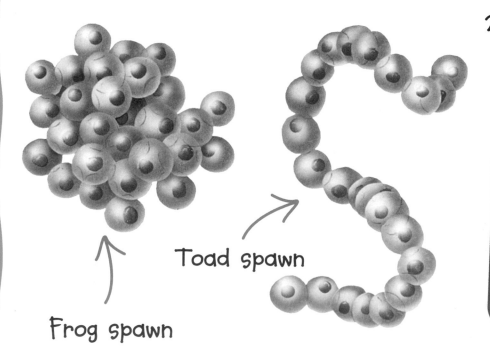

Frog spawn

Toad spawn

Look

In the spring, look carefully in a pond for frog spawn. Check it each day and you might see it hatch into tadpoles!

4. Adult frog

Danger in the air!

Frogs and toads have very good hearing. They also have good senses of taste and smell to check for signs of danger in the air around them.

Where do amphibians grow up?

Most amphibians are born and grow up in fresh water such as ponds, pools, streams, and rivers. They move onto dry land when they are adults and return to water to have their babies. This is called breeding. Most amphibians completely change their appearance as they grow.

3. Froglet

Which toad carries eggs on its back?

The female South American Surinam toad carries her eggs on her back. They are put there by her mate. The eggs stay on the mother's back until they hatch.

Where do reptiles lay their eggs?

Unlike amphibians, most reptiles lay their eggs on land. The eggs feed and protect the young inside them. The egg yolk provides food for the growing young. The shell protects the baby reptile from the outside world.

Crocodile laying eggs

Good luck!

A mother reptile only looks after her babies for a short time. Then they have to look after themselves. They must learn how to look for food and shelter very quickly.

Are reptile eggs strong?

Most reptile eggs are much tougher than those of amphibians. This is because they must survive life out of the water. Lizards and snakes lay eggs with leathery shells. Crocodile and tortoise eggs have a hard shell rather like birds' eggs.

Snake with eggs

Nest

Do baby crocodiles cry?

The baby Nile crocodile makes a very high-pitched noise, as if it's crying, when it is ready to hatch. Its mother then helps the baby to hatch by gently rolling the egg in her mouth.

Remember

Can you remember the two ways that an egg helps the young reptile growing inside it?

Are there tortoises in the desert?

Yes, there are. The desert tortoise is a shy reptile that lives in the sandy deserts of North America. It spends most of its time underground in the cool sand to escape the heat of the Sun. Adult desert tortoises can survive for about a year without water.

Desert tortoise

Are dragons real?

Early explorers told tales of dragons that lived in faraway lands. It may be that these explorers had seen giant lizards such as the Komodo dragon. These huge reptiles aren't really dragons at all!

Find

The Brazilian frog lives in Brazil in South America. Can you find Brazil on a map?

It's a boy...no!

A male baby alligator will develop in a warm egg, but a female baby alligator will develop in a cooler egg. For crocodiles, it's the other way around!

Can a frog sit on your finger?

One frog could! The Brazilian frog is less than 10 millimeters long and is small enough to sit on your thumbnail! The world's tiniest reptile is a type of lizard called a gecko. This lizard is less than 20 millimeters long.

Brazilian frog

Caribbean gecko

Why do lizards stick to walls?

Geckos can climb up walls or even walk upside down on ceilings. They are able to cling on because they have five wide-spreading toes, each with sticky toe-pads, on each foot. These strong pads are covered with millions of tiny hairs that grip surfaces tightly.

Why do chameleons have long tongues?

So they can catch their dinner. The chameleon keeps very still. When a tasty fly buzzes past, the chameleon catches it by quickly shooting out its long, sticky tongue and pulling the fly into its mouth.

Chameleon

Gecko

Pretend

Look in the mirror and stick out your tongue—pretend to be a chameleon catching a fly!

Which reptile can fly?

Flying geckos have webbed feet and folds of skin along their legs, tail, and sides. This means that they can fly, or glide, over short distances. They do this to either catch food, or to escape from danger.

Tight spot!

The chuckwalla lizard gets itself into tight corners. It can jam itself into a crack in a rock, then puff its body up so that enemies cannot pull it out.

Which lizard huffs and puffs?

The male anole lizard guards his home from other lizards in an unusual way. If other males come too close, he puffs out a bright red throat pouch at them. Two males may face each other with puffy throats for hours at a time!

Anole lizard

Show off!

A male newt goes to great lengths to impress a female during the mating season. He often has brightly colored skin, which he shows off to her!

Are lizards frilly?

The frilled lizard can be! This reptile has a large flap of skin that normally lies flat around its neck. When faced with danger, it spreads this skin out to form a huge, stiff neck frill that makes it look bigger and scarier!

Frilled lizard

Why do lizards show off their muscles?

Some male agamid lizards try to impress females with a little body-building. They can be seen perched on top of rocks, doing push-ups, and bobbing their heads up and down.

Think

Can you think of any other animals that have brightly colored skin, fur, or feathers?

Why do snakes stick out their tongues?

Snakes have poor hearing and eyesight. They use their tongue to "smell" the air for food or danger by constantly flicking it in and out. Rattlesnakes can sense heat given off by their prey, even in the dark.

Rattlesnake →

Count
Try to stare at something without blinking. Count how many seconds go by before you need to blink.

18

Can you see through a gecko?

One African gecko has very thin skin covering its ears. If you were to look at it with its ears lined up, you would be able to see light coming through from the other side of its head!

Strong shell!

A giant tortoise is so big and strong that it can support a one ton weight. This means that it could support a small car!

Iguana

Why can't iguanas blink?

Iguanas have very big eyes and good eyesight, but they cannot blink. Unlike humans, iguanas don't have movable eyelids. Instead of shutting their eyes to blink, they have special clear eyelids that sweep over their eyes to clean them.

Why do snakes squeeze their food?

Some snakes, like this ratsnake, kill their prey by squeezing it. They wrap their bodies around their meal and squeeze tightly until it stops breathing. Then the snake swallows the prey whole. After a big meal, the snake will not be hungry for a long time.

Why do snakes slither?

Unlike most reptiles, snakes do not have legs to help them move around. Instead they use powerful muscles in their bodies to push and pull themselves forward. Snakes are also covered in scales, which help them to grip the ground and slither along.

Measure

Using a tape measure, cut a piece of string 33 feet long. Lay it down outside to see how long a reticulated python can be!

Which snake is a copycat?

The milksnake pretends to be the coral snake by copying its colors. This is because the milksnake is not dangerous to bigger animals, but the coral snake is. Predators will not try to eat the coral snake because they are afraid of being bitten.

Ratsnake

Milksnake

King of snakes!

The longest snake in the world is the reticulated python, which grows up to 33 feet long. It could wrap its body around a person 12 times!

Which snake writes in the sand?

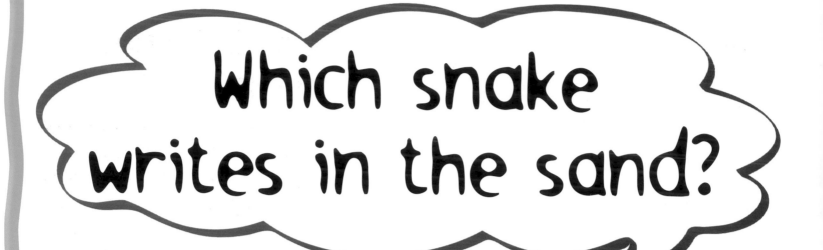

The sidewinding viper lives in the deserts of the United States. It moves along by pushing its body sideways against the sand, leaving a series of marks that are shaped like sideways letter Js. It does this so that its belly is not on the hot sand for too long.

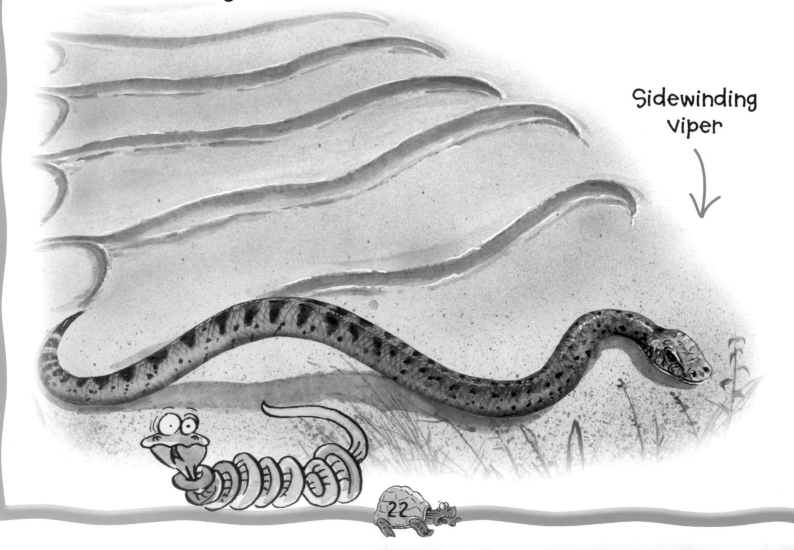

Sidewinding viper

Why do turtles swim so far?

To have their babies. Every two or three years, sea turtles may swim 620 miles to the beaches where they hatched to lay their eggs. Sea turtles have light, flat shells so they can swim easily under water.

Sea turtle

Can snakes live in water?

The floating sea snake can. Some fish swim close to the floating sea snake's tail to avoid being eaten. When the snake fancies a snack, it swims backward, fooling the unlucky fish into thinking its head is its tail!

Giants of the sea!

The largest turtle in the sea is called the leatherback turtle. It is 6.5 feet long—what a giant!

Swim

When you next go swimming, try to swim backward like a sea snake. Ask an adult to help you.

Are frogs dangerous?

Some are! Even one lick of the poison arrow frog would make a predator very ill. Its brightly colored skin warns enemies that it is poisonous and dangerous to eat.

Can a lizard's tail fall off?

Some lizards have detachable tails! If a hungry hunter grabs the tail of a five-lined tree skink lizard, it will be left just holding a twitching tail. The lizard can quickly run away and will grow back a new tail.

Think

Can you remember how long it takes a snake to shed all of its skin?

24

Poison arrow frog

Why do snakes shed their skin?

A snake's skin does not grow with its body. This means that it has to shed its old skin as it grows bigger. It can take about two weeks for a snake to shed its skin completely.

Grass snake shedding skin

Ready to burst!

A snake has to swallow food whole as it can't chew. It opens its jaws extra wide to gulp down animals much larger than itself.

Which lizard can run on two legs?

Fire-bellied toad

The crested water dragon from Asia can. In an emergency, this lizard can stand up on its back legs to run away from enemies. This is because it has large back feet and can run faster on two legs than on four over short distances.

Water dragon

Are toads colorful?

The fire-bellied toad has a bright red tummy. When it is threatened, the toad leaps away to safety, and the quick flash of red confuses its attacker and gives the frog more time to escape.

Sneaky hunters!

Crocodiles and alligators wait in shallow water for animals to come and drink, then they leap up and drag them under the water.

Play

How easy is it to sneak up on someone? See how quietly you can creep around the house without being noticed.

Do turtles play tricks?

The alligator snapper turtle looks like a rock as it lies on the ocean floor. The tip of its tongue looks like a juicy worm, which it waves at passing prey to tempt them into its jaws.

Do reptiles eat amphibians?

Some do. Most reptiles are meat eaters. The dwarf crocodile is so small that one frog is a big dinner. Frogs can jump very fast, but the dwarf crocodile snaps quickly at anything that makes a splash in the water near its jaws.

Dwarf crocodile

Are crocodiles always hungry?

After a big meal, a crocodile may not feel hungry again for a month or two. One of the most dangerous reptiles is the Nile crocodile. Each year it kills more people in Africa than lions do.

Think

How many different animals can you think of that have long, powerful tails?

Old lizard!

Some crocodiles are very old indeed. They can live to be over 100 years old. Crocodiles continue to grow throughout their lives.

Can crocodiles walk on their tails?

If they are being threatened, crocodiles can move so fast that they almost leap out of the water. This is called "tail-walking." Their tails are long and powerful, and they can kill with a single swipe.

Nile crocodiles

Quiz time

Do you remember what you have read about reptiles and amphibians? These questions will test your memory. The pictures will help you. If you get stuck, read the pages again.

3. Which toad carries eggs on its back?

page 9

4. Where do reptiles lay their eggs?

page 10

page 4

1. What is a reptile?

page 14

5. Why do chameleons have long tongues?

2. What is an amphibian?

page 5

6. Why do lizards show off their muscles?

page 17

30

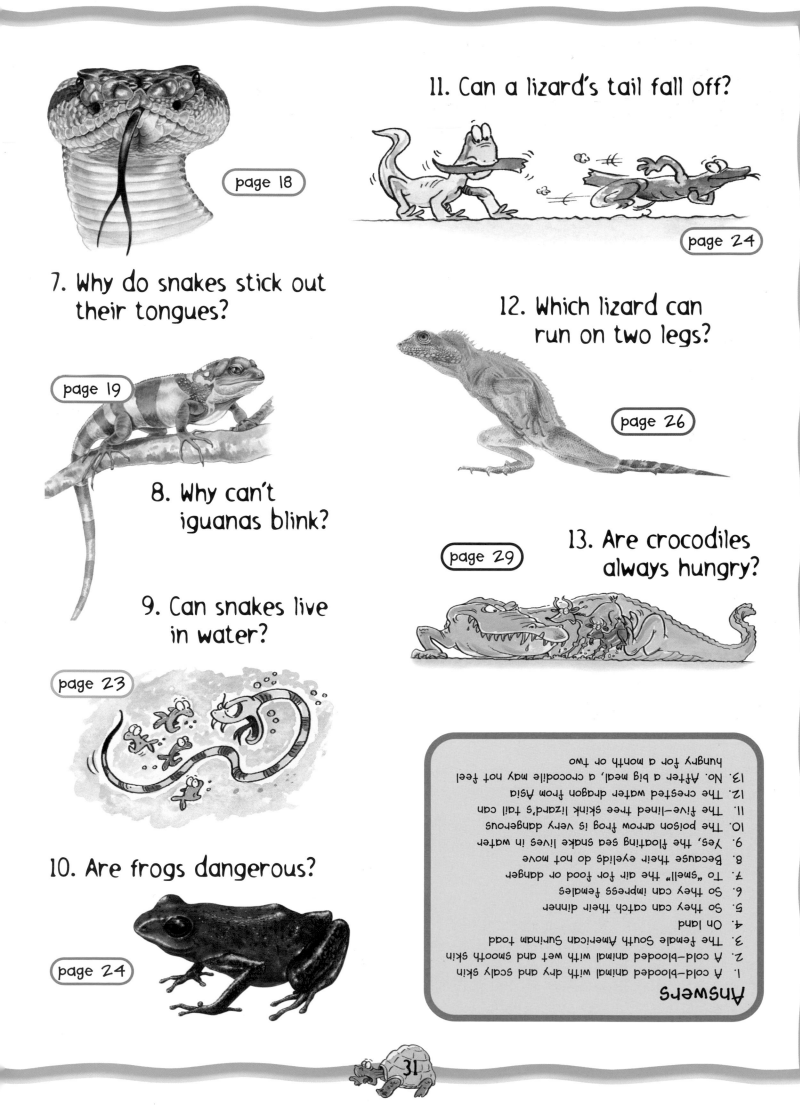

11. Can a lizard's tail fall off?

page 18

page 24

7. Why do snakes stick out their tongues?

page 19

12. Which lizard can run on two legs?

page 26

8. Why can't iguanas blink?

page 29

13. Are crocodiles always hungry?

9. Can snakes live in water?

page 23

10. Are frogs dangerous?

page 24

Answers

1. A cold-blooded animal with dry and scaly skin
2. A cold-blooded animal with wet and smooth skin
3. The female South American Surinam toad
4. On land
5. So they can catch their dinner
6. So they can impress females
7. To "smell" the air for food or danger
8. Because their eyelids do not move
9. Yes, the floating sea snake lives in water
10. The poison arrow frog is very dangerous
11. The five-lined tree skink lizard's tail can
12. The crested water dragon from Asia
13. No. After a big meal, a crocodile may not feel hungry for a month or two

Index